What a Coincidence!

What a Coincidence!

Margaret Hall

Copyright © 2011 Margaret Hall

The moral right of the author has been asserted.

Apart from any fair dealing for the purposes of research or private study, or criticism or review, as permitted under the Copyright, Designs and Patents Act 1988, this publication may only be reproduced, stored or transmitted, in any form or by any means, with the prior permission in writing of the publishers, or in the case of reprographic reproduction in accordance with the terms of licences issued by the Copyright Licensing Agency. Enquiries concerning reproduction outside those terms should be sent to the publishers.

Matador
9 Priory Business Park
Kibworth Beauchamp
Leicestershire LE8 0RX, UK
Tel: (+44) 116 279 2299
Fax: (+44) 116 279 2277
Email: books@troubador.co.uk
Web: www.troubador.co.uk/matador

ISBN 978-1848768-000

British Library Cataloguing in Publication Data.
A catalogue record for this book is available from the British Library.

Typeset in 12pt Adobe Garamond Pro by Troubador Publishing Ltd, Leicester, UK
Printed and bound in the UK by TJ International, Padstow, Cornwall

Matador is an imprint of Troubador Publishing Ltd

To Henry,
without whom none of these stories would have happened.

Contents

Acknowledgements	ix
Introduction	xi
Chapter 1. Across Salisbury Plain.	1
Chapter 2. Who is the Financial Prospector?	8
Chapter 3. A Tailor-Made Job.	15
Chapter 4. A Way of Escape.	19
Chapter 5. Unfulfilled.	24
Chapter 6. Meningitis Alert.	27
Chapter 7. Before You Call.	33
Chapter 8. The Umbrella.	36
Chapter 9. Little White Pet.	40
Chapter 10. A Sinking Feeling.	47
Chapter 11. The 'C' Word.	58
Chapter 12. Muscle-Wasting Disease.	62
Chapter 13. What Happened to July?	66
Chapter 14. Larger than Life	76
Chapter 15. A Shoulder Story	82
Chapter 16. Christmas	89

Acknowledgements

Grateful thanks are due to James, for his constant encouragement and advice during the writing of this book, and to Joy Tibbs and Ann Nixon for the time they have spent proof reading it.

Introduction

Everything in this book is true, as I see it. It is not meant to be a scientific research paper. I am just telling you what happened and it is up to you, the reader, to put your own interpretation on it. Each chapter is based around the time spent at South Chard Church. This story came long before that, when I was only a child. This event is of little significance in the grand scheme of things, but it had a profound effect on me as a child, and was instrumental in starting me on my life of faith. Faith is merely trusting in someone we can't see, but who we believe is there, and who wants to have a relationship with us.

This story starts at my favourite time of year. We were staying with granny and grandpa in their lovely chalet bungalow near Wimborne, Dorset. They slept downstairs, but all visitors slept in bedrooms in the loft. They had sloping walls, dormer-windows, fitted carpets and white washed walls. It seemed very exciting to Dilys, Enid and myself. Dilys was one of my sisters and she was was three years older than me, but two inches shorter, much to my satisfaction. However, what she lacked in size she made up for in personality.

Enid was our baby sister, being six years my junior, but she somehow managed to pass us both in height and carried it with great elegance.

We lived in the tiny village of Neyland, Pembrokeshire, in a bungalow that my father had had built in a field over looking the lovely Cleddau River, opposite Pembroke Dock. We had over half an acre of land around it, which sloped steeply and made cutting the grass hugely difficult for my father, but it meant it had a view to die for. Sometimes we had an animal in the field. Our most successful occupants were geese. Two geese and a gander to be accurate, called George, Gert and Daisy. They became reasonably tame and would race each other from the far side of the field to get to the food mum went out with. Sometimes they could not stop in time and would land beak over feet in a heap. Eventually they had to go. Mum had produced a beautiful garden and the birds did not contribute to its upkeep.

It was an idyllic childhood in many ways. My parents were both Quakers and could not have been more loving. My father, Stephen Griffith, was born in Blaenau Ffestiniog and spoke Welsh as his first language. He was now head of physics at Pembroke Grammar School so had every school holiday off and was able to take us to the beautiful Pembrokeshire beaches and teach us to swim. My mother, Clemency, came from Calne and taught domestic science until her children were born, but afterwards chose to be at home with us and was a brilliant cook. Both mum and dad were extremely hospitable to friends and neighbours alike, and anyone who came near was invited in for a meal, or at least a cup of tea and a flapjack.

We spent two weeks every summer with my grandparents. It was always a tiring journey from our home in Pembrokeshire. Sometimes we caught the train, which went through the long, dark Severn Tunnel, and my grandparents met us at Salisbury. On other occasions my father drove us. It was before the days of motorways or the Severn Bridge. We would take a picnic and eat it while waiting to catch the Aust Ferry. It was called the Severn Princess and it took us across the River Severn, from Wales to England. In those days it was a long day's journey.

In the summer of 1964 Dilys and Enid had both gone to a youth camp in Bala, so I went on my own with mum. Granny was very ill but I had no idea what was wrong. Such things were never discussed in front of the children. It was only later I found out that she had cancer, which had started as a cyst on her ovary but then spread throughout her body. All I knew was that she was in great pain and could not sleep at night. She had become very thin, her arms poking out of her blouse looked like sticks that might snap if I lent against them, although her tummy was huge with water retention. She was unable to walk and she sat in a wheelchair.

One night I was in the bedroom on my own. It seemed terrible to me that someone who was as wonderful and loving as granny, should suffer so. As a child, I did not know whether God was able to do anything about it, or would even want to. But I did something I had never done before. I got down on my knees and pleaded with God.

'Please God,' I said, 'give granny the best night's sleep since all this trouble started.' And with that I got into bed and slept peacefully.

The next morning I was woken by my mother coming in with a jug of warm water, which she poured into a matching earthenware bowl for me to wash in. After hurriedly washing and dressing, I ran down stairs to the smell of warm toast. Granny was sitting downstairs waiting for me, with her usual cheerful smile.

'How did you sleep, granny?' I asked.

'Well, do you know,' she replied, 'I had the best night's sleep since all this trouble started!'

I was too shocked at her reply to say anything. She had used the exact same words that I had used in my prayer. I silently thanked God that He had heard me. This was to be the foundation for the rest of my life, and indeed the rest of this book.

Granny died peacefully soon afterwards.

Uncle Sid and Auntie Mill

Chapter One

Across Salisbury Plain

The sky was velvet black, with hardly a star to be seen as we drove along the A30, across Salisbury plain. We had quite a way to go before we joined the A303. It was the early hours of the morning and we were returning to West Drayton in Middlesex, after a weekend of meetings at the South Chard Church, which was an old barn conversion, hidden in a little village on the Devon-Somerset border.

South Chard Church was one of the pioneer churches of the Charismatic Movement. It was started by Sid and Millie Purse as a small house church in the front room of their home, the Manor House, which was a large, white, rambling old thatched house built in the sixteenth century. It officially opened in 1956 in the church that Sid had built from their old coach house. By the middle of the 1960s it had become known all over the world, and people travelled in their hundreds to experience the moving of the Holy Spirit. Henry Hall and I became engaged in 1970, and we formed our own house group in West Drayton with Michael and Eileen Hornsby, among others. We travelled down to South Chard on regular occasions in order to join in with these meetings and to enjoy the ministry of Harry Greenwood, Ian Andrews and other wonderful speakers who had by now joined 'Uncle Sid', as he became known.

On that particular Sunday evening, the meeting had finished at about eleven o'clock, and afterwards we all crowded into Auntie Mill's kitchen for a cup of her home-made soup, before we set out on the three-and-a-half-hour journey home. The kitchen was filled by her large frame and hearty laugh as she ladled out the soup. She towered over Uncle Sid, but what he lacked in size he made up for in Spirit.

Henry, our friends, Michael and Eileen, and I were in the car driving home.

'What did you think of the weekend?' I asked the other three.

'The meetings were awesome,' Henry admitted. 'I wished we lived nearer and could go more often.'

'The Manor House seems to have elastic walls. I don't know how Aunty Mill fitted everyone in,' Eileen added.

'Not that it was a rest, mind you.' Michael said. 'She knows how to utilise the workforce sleeping in her beds.' He fidgeted with his long thin legs behind my seat and moved them into a more comfortable position.

We chatted enthusiastically about the weekend we had just shared with dozens of others who had stayed in the Manor House. Saturday morning was the time for preparing the vegetables for Sunday dinner and we had peeled bucket loads of potatoes. She catered for about a hundred guests for Sunday dinner, and her roast potatoes and meat pies were legendary. The meetings on Saturday and Sunday had been great and very exciting. We tried to recall all that had happened.

We also discussed our forthcoming wedding. Henry and I were getting married the next May at South Chard. Michael was an ordained Baptist minister and would marry us. Eileen was an organist and would play for us. Henry's best man would be Eric James, who was his lodger at West Drayton. The plans were beginning to take shape.

The roads were deserted as Henry drove across the plain and we were making good progress. We should be home before three in the morning at this rate.

All of a sudden, the car lights dimmed and went out altogether. The car whimpered and stuttered to a standstill. Complete darkness enclosed us and the silence was deafening.

'I'll get the tools from the boot,' said Henry cheerily, as he swung his legs out of the car.

He came back a few moments later looking very sheepish.

'I remember now that I took them out for the MOT and service before the weekend, and I forgot to put them back. All I've found is a torch.'

'What a prize idiot,' barked Michael. 'What are we supposed to do now. I've got to be in work first thing in the morning.'

'Could we start walking?' I suggested. 'We might see a house and get help from there.'

'No point,' answered Michael, sounding very disgruntled.' People would be asleep at this time of night, and even if we woke them up, no garage would be open to come and rescue us.'

We were totally marooned. We stood there shivering in the cool night air. At least it was not raining, but it could be a long night if we had to wait for a garage to open and for someone to come out to rescue us. Of course we were all supposed to be at work later that day, but it didn't look as if that would happen now. It was before the days of mobile phones and we were unable to contact anyone for help. The traffic had been sparse as we had travelled along earlier; now the road was completely empty. There was only deep darkness all around.

'Do you have any blankets in the car to keep us warm until daylight?' asked Eileen, her curly hair waving gently in the breeze as she spoke.

'No, we have nothing.' admitted Henry.

Desperation began to grip us as we realised the plight we were in.

'We could pray.' suggested Eileen helpfully.

We all looked at her doubtfully.

'You pray and we'll say Amen,' agreed Michael.

So we did.

With that, a car's headlights appeared in the distance. We got ready to wave the driver down with our torch, and as he reached us, we saw he was driving an old white Ford E83W van. The driver pulled over onto the other side of the road and a young man, probably in his thirties, got out of the driving seat. He was casually dressed, in jeans and a sweater and was on his own. He walked over to us at a leisurely pace and asked whether he could help us. We explained our predicament.

'That's ok, I'm a racing car mechanic,' he explained, and showed us inside the back of his van. He had every type of tool that you could possibly need stored in there. He looked under the bonnet of our car and quickly saw what the trouble was – a loose fan belt. He rummaged around in his van, hunting for the right tools, and soon returned triumphantly.

'What are you doing driving across Salisbury Plain at this time of night?' we asked him.

'Nothing,' he said. 'I just decided to go for a drive.'

'But where are you going?' we persisted, feeling amazed.

'Nowhere,' he replied, showing no embarrassment at his strange decision. I'm going home now.'

We were astonished. It seemed so unlikely to us.

Our car was soon running again and we could not thank him enough for his help. He said his goodbyes and before we could engage him in any more conversation he drove off. We were able to finish our long journey with no more interruptions, but with very thankful hearts.

Across Salisbury Plain

The Manor House

Chapter Two

Who is the Financial Prospector?

In 1971 we started to panic. Had we done the right thing by signing for a house in Chard before we had sold our house at West Drayton?

Both Henry and I thought God had spoken to us and told us to move. We also thought God had said 'February'. So in the autumn of 1971, we drove to an estate agent in Chard and put our cross on a plot of land that was to be built on, in an area called Ashcroft. It was to be a three-bedroomed semi-detached house. When we returned to West Drayton, we put our house on the market, expecting it to be sold quite quickly. It was a 1930's semi-detached house with three bedrooms and bay windows, which Henry had modernised and decorated throughout. It had a large garden, front and back. Henry had built a beautiful rose arch which separated the back lawn from the vegetable garden. It was only half a mile from Heathrow Airport, but it was not under a flight path, so was relatively quiet. The estate agent thought it would be a very sought-after property.

A few weeks later, we had a phone call from Margaret Joy who worked at the Chard estate agents.

'Your Chard house is going to double in price next week. If you want it at the present price, you'll have to sign for it this weekend,' she explained.

So, once again, we drove down to Chard, along the now familiar A30, winding our way through the pretty villages that dotted the route. It was late summer and the hedgerows were passed their best, even the hanging baskets were looking a little jaded. But the sun was shining and nothing could dampen our spirits as we drove along. It felt like going home as we approached Chard.

Our first call was to the estate agent where we paid our deposit and signed for the house that was to be ours, although the builders had not even started on it by this time.

Now we knew we would have to sell quickly. Once the Chard house was built, the contractors would want their money straight away. However, our West Drayton home would not sell. We tried selling it through agents. We tried advertising it privately. Still nothing. February was drawing closer and we began to feel fear creeping in. Perhaps we had been foolish to sign up for the new house. Would we end up with a huge bridging loan we could not afford to repay?

February of 1972 came and went. We must have

been mistaken about hearing from God. The months rolled by and still our house did not sell, but neither did our Chard house get built. Every time we visited it, there was just a plot of land with nothing on it. We could not work out what was happening.

For those that remember that year, you may also remember it was the year of soaring house prices. By the end of the year the house in Ashcroft was being built, and our West Drayton house was sold – for almost double its original price. Meanwhile, our Ashcroft house was pegged at half the price of the semi which was attached to it. We could not have organised that ourselves if we had tried!

We moved into our new house in February 1973! The thing we had not asked God was which February He had meant!

We were very content in our Ashcroft home. Henry had five months off work before he found a job, so he was able to do quite a bit of work on it, particularly on the garden where he laid a patio, lawn and flowerbeds. He was very practical, having been an engineer in his younger days, so his arms were muscular and strong and he tackled the jobs that needed doing in the house with enthusiasm.

We soon made many friends amongst the members of South Chard Church, and one day I was invited to a coffee morning at the home of Tony and Janet Nash, who lived in St Mary's Crescent, not far from us. I walked through their back gate and into their large garden. It was lovely. I admired their rows of runner beans and noticed their flourishing apple trees. There were two Cox's. What a treat! When I walked in through the front door I was immediately struck by a feeling of peace. I walked around the rooms downstairs and just loved it. I walked back home to Henry later and told him about it.

'That's a house I would love to own one day,' I said.

Tony, a little cockney Jew with a big sense of humour, was a minister at our church, and Janet, a delightful English lady, had her hands full looking after their four young children. They were well settled in Chard, and so were we. There were always things to do at home, and, with us both working, and our involvement in church, there was little time to think of anything else.

Eighteen months later, Henry came home one day and told me that Tony and Janet were moving to America and their house was on the market. We looked at each other.

'I'm not sure I want to move from our lovely Ashcroft house,' I replied.

'Well I don't suppose we could afford it anyway, but it wouldn't do any harm to look at the details,' he said.

We walked down to the estate agent where Margaret Joy worked and we asked for the details. We took the sheet home and studied it. We decided the price was too high for us. With that, the telephone rang. It was Margaret Joy.

'I have a couple here who want to buy your house. Can they visit you this afternoon, please?'

'But we haven't decided to sell yet,' we gasped.

"Well let them look. You don't have to make a decision now."

We had a mad dash around trying to tidy up, pushing our clutter into cupboards and under cushions. Then they arrived. We showed them round and again explained we had not decided anything.

When they had gone we sat down and took stock. What should we do? We talked for some time before coming to a decision. If God wanted us to move, then the couple would agree to the full asking price of our house. We would put an offer in on Tony and Janet's house that we could afford, taking into account the money we had made when we moved down from West Drayton. We phoned Margaret Joy and gave her our offer.

The next day we had a phone call from Margaret Joy.

'The couple have agreed to the full asking price, and Tony and Janet have agreed to accept your offer,' she told us.

Who is the Financial Prospector?

We were amazed that the whole thing had happened within twenty-four hours, and decided that this was confirmation of God's will. We moved a short time after that, and still live in that house thirty-seven happy years later.

What a Coincidence!

South Chard Church, 2011

Chapter Three

A Tailor-Made Job

'Good afternoon,' said Henry to the tall, middle-aged man standing on the other side of the counter. 'Can I help you?'

Henry worked at Lloyds Bank in Hayes in 1971. He worked on one of the tills and enjoyed meeting the customers who came in. It was a busy branch and he got to know the regular customers who paid frequent visits.

He had been a late entrant into the bank, having done a five-year apprenticeship in heavy engineering. He become an inspector at Power Plant Gears, but he had got bored with it. He did accountancy 'O' level and 'A' level and then applied to the bank. He was accepted and found he enjoyed the work, especially meeting the customers.

This particular customer was one he had not seen before. As he dealt with his request, he asked where he was from.

'From Chard, a little town in Somerset,' he replied, thinking that Henry would not have heard of it.

'Oh, I'm moving there soon,' said Henry.

'Well, my name is Allen Elliott and I'm the chief engineer of a company in Chard called Space Decks. If you ever need a job, contact me. Here's my card.'

Henry thanked him and put the card in his pocket.

It turned out to be two years later that we moved to Chard. The banks have a policy of not transferring anyone out of London, so Henry was unable to continue working for a bank once we had moved. He was unemployed for five months, which was quite useful as our house was new and needed plenty of work to make it homely, especially the garden.

One day Henry was looking through the window of the Job Centre when he saw an advert for an office job at Space Decks. He walked in and enquired about the card in the window. No one knew anything about it. They admitted they did not know who had placed it there. They phoned up Space Decks to find out more. No one at Space Decks knew anything about it either. They did not know who had sent the advert to the Job Centre, as they had no job vacancy. They were sorry they could not help. Everyone was mystified.

Henry was puzzling over this advert when suddenly he remembered Mr Elliott. What had he done with the card he was given two years ago? He reached into his pocket and there it was, still in his wallet. He gave Mr. Elliott a ring.

'I'm Henry Hall,' he announced. 'Do you remember meeting me in Lloyds Bank, Hayes, two years ago?'

Amazingly, he remembered it well, and was interested in Henry's encounter with the Job Centre.

'I'll make enquiries and get back to you,' he responded.

A few days later he rang.

'Come along tomorrow, and the managing director will interview you,' he announced.

Space Decks was quite easy to find, and he drove in through the main gates. There was a man on duty in the little gate hut, so Henry asked him for directions.

'Turn left, drive a hundred yards and you'll see some old huts on the right. They look like old army huts and they should have been pulled down years ago. That's where you'll find the managing director,' he replied.

Henry found it to be just as the man had described and the M.D. was there in his office, busily going through his papers. He greeted Henry warmly, and they sat down together, discussing accounts. After they had chatted for a little while, Henry was offered a job.

'There isn't a vacancy in any of the other departments at the moment,' he said, 'but if you come in next week, you can work for me.'

Henry was given the position of costing clerk, reporting directly to Mr Gray.

He retired from Space Decks twenty-eight years later, having worked his way through every department in the firm.

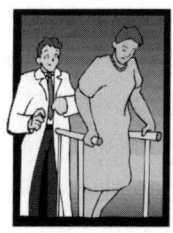

Chapter Four

A Way of Escape

It was Monday morning again and I did not want to get out of bed. I had a difficult journey to the Axminster Centre where I worked, and it was the worst job I had ever done. I hated it. All day, every day. Don't get me wrong, it was a good job – I was in a senior position as a full-time and well-paid occupational therapist. But I was really miserable. It was the first job I had been able to find since moving to Chard. The clients were adults with learning difficulties and I loved every one of them, but the staff, who had all been there for the ten years since the centre had opened, made it obvious that I was not wanted there. It was a day centre within a complex of small residential homes, and my boss worked in Exeter, thirty miles away. He never phoned me to ask how it was going. He only visited me once in three months, and that was to give me a list of complaints. To make matters worse, the person in charge at the complex was married to one of the women at the day centre, where I was in charge. There was nobody I could talk to. I was left floundering on my own and felt very inadequate.

When talking to Uncle Sid about it, he would only say, 'It's all good, lover.' By way of explanation, he would add: 'There's no problem outside of yourself. It's your reactions that God wants right.'

That made me think. After all, I could sing and rejoice with everyone else on Sunday. Should I not be doing the same on Monday morning? Or was I being hypocritical by living a life of double standards? I decided I would praise God whatever happened.

The next Monday I went to work early. Before anyone else had arrived, I started to sing praises to God and to thank Him for His goodness to me. I continued to do this each morning. The result of all this praise and thanksgiving was that the situation became worse! In fact, it became so bad that a meeting was called by management to discuss the problem. The meeting descended into a slanging match and I was devastated. I left with my tail between my legs, and as I called to God in desperation, a verse suddenly popped into my head: "God is faithful, who will not allow you to be tested more than you are able; but will, with the test, also make a way of escape, so that you may be able to bear it." (1 Corinthians chapter 10, verse 13).

'God, I need a way of escape,' I cried.

When I reached home, Henry had just brought in the Chard and Ilminster News, our local newspaper.

'Can I have a look after you?' I asked him. He threw it over to me.

'Not much in it this week,' he commented.

I looked through the 'job vacancies' page with a heavy heart. I felt like taking anything. Perhaps I could stack shelves in the supermarket. Or I could try the Oscar Mayer factory down the road. Lots of people did it.

As I looked down the page, an advert leapt out at me. There, written in bold letters, was a job advert for an occupational therapist at Chard Hospital, which was right opposite where Henry worked. I could hardly believe my eyes! The role was rehabilitating elderly patients before they were discharged – my ideal job. I had done it many times before and loved it, and there would be no more awkward journeys as I could go into work by car with Henry. I knew it was my job, I was so thrilled. There was only one problem. My present job was a full-time senior position whereas this job was basic grade and was for only ten hours a week. The drop in pay would be enormous and we still had our mortgage to pay. However, I knew that this was God's 'way of escape' for me and trusted that God would provide. I applied for the job and the next day I handed in my notice at Axminster.

Each day I looked expectantly on the doormat for a letter calling me for interview. A month came and went. No letter. Surely they could not have had the interviews without me. Perhaps they had already appointed someone. Perhaps someone wanted a transfer from another hospital. Should I look for another job?

Eventually the phone rang. It was the head occupational therapist at Taunton. She was apologetic. She had been off sick and, now Christmas was approaching, the interviews were being postponed until the new year. I would get a letter in a few weeks. I felt relieved and deflated at the same time. All this waiting about was making me anxious. I needed a job. I hoped I had not been foolhardy leaving the Day Centre.

Eventually I was called for interview at Musgrove Park Hospital in Taunton and turned up in my smartest outfit, with my hair done up specially for the occasion. I did not want to let myself down at this stage. I was grilled by the head occupational therapist and a senior manager. They asked me about my past jobs, my experience and my knowledge. I felt at perfect peace. Eventually, they offered me the job. No surprise there, then. What did surprise me was the next sentence.

' We have been given extra funding for this post.'

That is something that does not normally happen in the NHS!

'We have decided to upgrade the position to a senior grade, and to increase the hours to however many you would like to do.'

My mouth must have dropped open before I composed myself. I accepted the job with pleasure and told them how many hours I would like to work.

It turned out to be one of the most enjoyable jobs I have had, and never again did I find going to work on Monday mornings a problem.

Chapter Five

Unfulfilled

Another month came and I had not fallen pregnant. I was devastated. Henry and I had been married for four years already and we were desperate for children. Neither of us were young anymore and time was passing us by. That night I got on my knees before God.

'Why me, Lord? Why am I different from everyone else? Why can't I be a mum?'

The answer came back swiftly and clearly.

'I have a perfect plan for all your children. If they are born at the wrong time then they will have the wrong friends, the wrong teachers, the wrong circumstances.'

I was staggered by this. It was so unexpected.

'How can I know that I really am going to have children?' I asked God. 'I just want to know. Please tell me.'

I then did something I had never done before or since. And it certainly is not something I would recommend as a general rule. But I was desperate.

'I shall open the Bible at random, Lord, and point my finger at a verse. If I am going to have children, may it be a verse about them, please?'

I opened the Bible and with my eyes shut I stabbed my finger onto the page. I looked at it. It was Isaiah chapter 7, verse 14: "A young woman will conceive a child! She will give birth to a son." For a moment my heart stopped.

'Was that verse a coincidence, Lord?' I asked. 'Can You do it again, to make sure?'

I repeated the process, placing my finger on a different place in the Bible. Again the verse was about the birth of a child.

'Can You do it just one more time, please Lord?' The result was the same. At last I was convinced. I gave God thanks and, from that time on, I remained in peace, despite the lack of evidence.

One day Owen Keitch, a church elder at South Chard, and his wife, Margaret, called on us. He started to pray for me and prayed that God would bring everything in my body into order, and make it work correctly. I knew that God had done something in me but I had no idea what.

Nine months later, in 1976, our first son, James, was born.

We wanted to enlarge our family and, assuming we would have no more trouble conceiving, looked forward to our next baby. Nothing happened. Five years came and went. Still nothing. However, I felt such assurance that it was all a matter of God's timing that I didn't fret. Then one day Norman Hawkins, another elder at South Chard, and his wife, Molly, came to us with a message about us having another baby. They prayed for us and nine months later Peter arrived.

Although we felt fulfilled with our two boys, the arrival of Susy a couple of years later delighted us both. They are all wonderful gifts from the Lord, and I thank Him everyday for giving them to us.

Chapter Six

Meningitis Alert

It was a warm Saturday afternoon in 1980 and Henry was digging up the potatoes ready for the next day's Sunday roast. We had my sister, Enid, and brother-in-law, David, staying with us. We also had our four-year-old son, James, and our little foster girl, Michelle, who was only a month old.

Michelle was our second foster baby. Our first had been a little boy called Alan. We had picked him up from Musgrove Hospital when he was ten days old, after his mother had decided she could not keep him. We had looked after him and loved him for six weeks before the couple who were going to adopt him came to fetch him. They were ecstatic that their dream of having a baby was finally coming true. It made the weeks of sleepless nights we had endured so worthwhile. We spent a happy day together while I showed them how to feed, bath and change the little chap. Some months later we collected Michelle from

Musgrove when she was just a week old. She was really tiny and so sweet. She had been with us a month and I loved her dearly. She had skin problems, but I had special cream to rub into her skin, so we were managing well.

This particular Saturday Henry began to feel faint and giddy.

'I think perhaps I've been doing too much gardening or I've been out in the sun for too long. I don't feel too well. I'm going to call it a day and have a lie down,' he explained, as he struggled indoors and lay down on the settee. We were watching the television and he tried to follow the story. It was about a virus that was sweeping the country and killing the people off.

'This is making me feel worse', he announced. 'I'm going to bed.'

I went up with him to check he was alright. His eyes had been feeling 'prickly' all week, as if there was grit in them, and now he was feeling hot and sweaty and looked grey, so I helped him into bed.

That night is a complete blank to him. He was restless and kept falling out of bed and groaning. In the morning, I put James on the church minibus to go off to Sunday School, then went back up to see Henry. I got him out of bed so I could remake it. Suddenly, he started shaking and I realised he was having an epileptic fit. He collapsed on the floor.

After getting him back into bed, I rang two people. First I phoned the doctor and then Harry Greenwood, a man who was larger than life, both in stature and in personality. Harry arrived first, with his son, David. They prayed for Henry's complete healing and then the duty doctor arrived.

He examined him and said to me, 'He has meningitis. Can I use your phone? I need to call for an ambulance'.

It arrived within ten minutes and the two burly paramedics carried him downstairs on a stretcher and out to the waiting ambulance. They were dressed in protective clothing as meningitis is so infectious. He was taken to Musgrove Hospital in Taunton with the blue lights flashing and the sirens blaring all the way.

Meanwhile, Harry went to church and asked them to pray. I had to dash off to follow the ambulance and so was unable to see to the two children. However, David had a car and was able to pick James up from Sunday School, and Enid was a midwife and was able to look after the baby wonderfully. What a coincidence that they were there just when I needed them!

Henry was put into a side room on his own and barrier-nursed. The curtains were closed as the light was hurting his eyes. There was a fan on his locker, blowing towards him in order to keep him cool. His dark, wiry hair waved at me each time the fan turned in his direction. It was the only thing that moved. The rest of him lay motionless on the hard hospital bed. I sat in the chair beside him on my own and wondered what was to become of him. I had heard such scare stories about people with meningitis and felt afraid. What was I going to do if Henry was taken from me? I had a little four-year-old boy at home. Would he grow up without a father? I had no mobile phone with which to phone anyone. I felt very alone.

He was visited by several doctors. First in was the houseman. She wrote down his particulars as I related all the proceedings of the day.

She wiggled his toes and asked him, "Which way am I moving them?"

Henry grunted a response, but seemed unsure what she was talking about. She examined his reflexes, looked in his eyes and studied his skin. She showed me his back.

'Look. He has a typical meningeal rash,' she commented. He did have a nasty red rash right across his back. I had not noticed that before. The registrar was the next to come in. He repeated the tests, even wiggled his toes again and asked which way he was moving them. Henry was no more responsive than before. I explained about the feeling of grit he had had in his eyes all week.

'That is one of the symptoms,' he explained.

In the evening the consultant arrived. All the tests were repeated, and again Henry had his toes wiggled. They all confirmed he had a typical case of meningitis. He lay there all day, not speaking and not eating.

The next morning Harry and Pam Greenwood came back and prayed for him again. They were both Irish, and Harry towered over Pam as they stood by his bed. They knew he was seriously ill. The doctors did a lumbar puncture, taking off some spinal fluid to test for meningitis. With my sister and brother-in-law still at home, looking after the children, I was able to spend the day with Henry once more. He had to lie still and flat on his back all day. He did not speak and I sat there in silence, in the darkened room, waiting for the results. I stayed there, alone with my dark thoughts, all day. The results did not come until the evening.

'The test was negative!'

The registrar gave me the good news. He told me that there was no sign of meningitis in his body at all! I hurried home to tell everyone..

When I visited Henry on Tuesday he was sitting up eating a roast dinner and wondering what all the fuss was about. When I asked the consultant about it, he had no idea.

'It was an electrical phenomenon,' he said to me.

Henry enjoyed the rest of the week. He was able to eat all the food they gave him, have plenty of visitors and be generally spoiled. They sent him home at the end of the week, completely well.

The only symptom he has left, to remind us of God's wonderful healing, is scar tissue on his eyes, and even now, whenever he has his eyes tested, they still remark on it.

Chapter Seven

Before You Call

I waved goodbye to my eldest son, James, as he trotted off to school with a friend's mother, his satchel hanging off his shoulder. He was eight years old and he waved cheerily back at me. I put on my best smile for him, hoping that he would not have dropped his lunch out of his bag before he reached school. He was fairly laid-back about most things, but I knew that if he had nothing to eat at lunch time, it would be a major catastrophe as far as he was concerned.

It was a glorious June day and, as he disappeared round the corner, I could hear the blackbirds singing their brightest melody, as if to serenade him on his way.

I closed the door and my smile disappeared. I looked up at the stairs that I needed to climb. There were only thirteen of them, but I did not know how I was going to make it up to the top. It was nearly nine o'clock in the morning and I was still in my dressing gown.

I was seven months pregnant with Susy, and I had

been really well with my previous two pregnancies. This time was different. I had not felt well for some time but I put it down to my age – after all, I was thirty seven. I also had my second son, Peter, a two-year-old toddler, who was the epitome of perpetual motion and who had a determination like steel. He was blond and blue-eyed and had a smile that lit up the room. He was my sunshine and showers boy and had the most infectious laugh, but when he cried, the whole neighbourhood knew! He was still in his pyjamas and his nappy must have been saturated, but I did not have the energy to deal with him. I felt depressed, bad-tempered and unable to cope. Henry could do nothing right and, when he was not working, I took my misery out on him.

At that moment I called to God. 'I cannot cope any longer,' I cried. 'Please send someone to help me.'

With that, there was a ring at the door bell. Who could be calling on me so early, I wondered? It was not yet nine o'clock. I opened the door. It was my friend Stephanie Cockerill, with her baby son, David, in her arms. She looked, as she always did, immaculate in hair and dress. I had known Steph since she was seventeen, when she came to live with us for a short while. It was now ten years later and she was married to Andrew with twin eight-year-old boys, Stephen and Darren, and a three- month-old baby.

'I've come to see if I can give you any help,' she said, smiling warmly at me and showing no shock at my dishevelled appearance.

I was momentarily speechless. Then I burst into tears. She had been on her way to me before I even called to God. The verse sprang into my mind, "Before they call I will answer." (Isaiah chapter 65, verse 24.)

She packed me off to bed.

'You stay there for the day,' she ordered. 'I'll sort everything out.'

She washed and dressed Pete, cleaned the house and cooked a dinner for Henry and I to have later. When she had finished, she took Pete back to her own house while I slept. She had no car at the time, so had to push Pete and David together in the pushchair. What a friend! And what a God!

I was soon diagnosed as having severe anaemia, treated with iron tablets and became almost human again.

Chapter Eight

The Umbrella

'Can I come with you, mummy?' Susy pleaded.

'Not today, darling. Mrs Turner wants to see the parents on their own. I'll tell you what she said when I get back and if you have been a good girl, I'll give you a special prize.'

It was a beautiful, sunny afternoon in June, with hardly a cloud in the sky as I walked with Susy down the road. She would play with her friend, Adele, while I talked with her teacher. For some reason I had picked up my telescopic umbrella as I walked out of the house and now found it a nuisance. Still, it was too late to take it back. I just hoped I wouldn't leave it behind at the school later.

I enjoyed walking past the gardens of the Manor Farm houses. They were a symphony of colour at this time of year and I breathed in the the scented air with pleasure. I admired the sweet rocket, irises and columbine, with an occasional early rose catching my eye. There was a copper beech tree which I loved and it had become hazily pink with tiny leaves. Susy chatted continuously to me until I left her with Adele then I continued down the school lane. It was narrow, with a sharp bend in it as it bordered the school playground. That side had a high fence and on the other side was a grassy patch and bushes from where I could hear a blackbird singing its little heart out. At the start and finish of school, the lane teamed with small bodies rushing along in higgledy piggledy groups. Now it was empty, except for the occasional parent, grimly marching to hear their judgment.

It only took me five minutes to reach Susy's classroom where I was meeting her reception teacher, to see how she had settled into her first year. Mrs Turner beamed at me.

'Do sit down,' she said.

I squeezed my rather large bottom onto the tiny reception chair and sat with a questioning look on my face.

'It's all good news,' she informed me as she passed me the written report. 'Susy is a bright girl, full of enthusiasm and a delight to teach.'

'What about her behaviour?' I enquired.

'I've no complaints there, either,' she replied. 'She has lovely manners and tries hard to please.'

I glowed with pride. What more could I ask for?

'Her year's work is all here,' she added, passing me a box of books. 'Look through it at your leisure.'

She moved on to the next parent and I lost myself in Susy's books and pictures. There were lots of attempts at writing, and some of her spellings made me laugh. 'The bik cow had blak and wit spats,' she wrote. But it wasn't bad for a five year old. Her number work had hardly got off the ground and her pictures were a complete mystery. In fact I would not have known what they were if the teacher had not neatly labelled them. She was obviously no budding Constable! Her reading books about 'Billy Blue Hat' were familiar to me as she brought them home regularly. It was all very satisfactory.

I was wending my way back up the lane with a song in my heart, when a lad ran past. He was tall, about sixteen or seventeen, I guessed, and dressed in the smart casual look of his generation. He ran ahead of me, round the corner. As I reached the bend in the lane, I saw he was stooped down, tying his shoe laces. Thinking nothing of it, I walked briskly past him.

At that moment he made a grab for my legs, reaching inside my skirt, and he clung on. It all happened so quickly. I wasn't prepared for it, but my reaction was instant. I hit him hard on the head, over and over again, with my umbrella. It seemed an age before he released his grip, got up and ran off back down the lane. I was left standing there very shaken. I walked a few yards and was sick. But I was proud of myself. I had not frozen to the spot and become a victim, as I imagined I would, but had risen to the occasion and fought back.

'Thank you God for the umbrella,' I murmured quietly.

Henry was still at work when I returned home, but my neighbour, Peter Miller, was in and, as I related my story to him, he bundled me into his car and took me down to the police station. The sergeant immediately drove us around Chard, up and down the main streets and round the estates looking for him, without success.

It was some weeks later he was caught – attempting to strangle a woman who was out in the fields walking her dog. When he was brought before the court, he asked for five other offenses to be taken into consideration, including mine.

Chapter Nine

Little White Pet

'Please, please, please can I have a West Highland White?' wailed Susy.

'No, no, no!' I replied. 'For the hundredth time, no! Dogs are a tie, they are expensive to keep and take a lot of looking after.'

'But I'll do everything for it, honestly. I'll feed it, walk it, brush it, play with it. You won't have to do a thing.'

That night I talked to Henry. Susy was fourteen, and maybe the responsibility of a dog would be good for her. I was under no illusion about how long the enthusiasm of her looking after a dog would last. I knew I would end up doing most of the work, but perhaps we should consider it.

In addition, the boys had left home, so Susy was on her own. James had not returned since leaving for university. Now he was working for a firm in Cheltenham, writing computer software. Pete, on the other hand, was sailing the high seas. He had been on the Tall Ships Race from Falmouth to Lisbon that summer, after leaving school, and loved it so much that he had joined the Ocean Youth Club and crewed up and down the rivers of Holland.

We prayed that God would show us if it was right to get a dog. The next morning I chatted to Susy about it. I told her that I would ring up all the animal sanctuaries in the area and see if any of them had a Westie. I wouldn't pay for a pedigree. And it would have to be a bitch.

That day I rang Ferne Animal Sanctuary.

'Do you have a West Highland White among your rescue dogs?' I enquired.

'Oh, no,' the lady said, 'We never get Westies in. They are too popular a dog and they have nice temperaments.'

I thanked her and phoned up West Hatch RSPCA centre. I asked the same question. Her reply was adamant. They had never had a Westie. I next phoned Heaven's Gate near Langport.

'Not a chance,' she pronounced. 'However, we are open to the public and we do have some very nice dogs that need re-homing. Why don't you come and look round?'

I was working as a community occupational therapist at the time in the Langport area, so one lunch time I decided to have a look round. I paid my one pound entrance fee and went into reception. They had a board there with the photos of sixty dogs and a full description of their personalities. I read each one, but none sounded slightly interesting to me. I decided to walk round the centre.

I had just started walking up the hill when I heard a voice behind me say, 'Look, there's a little Westie.'

I stopped in my tracks and spun round. Two elderly ladies were looking over a wall into the quarantine area. I ran back to see what they were looking at. There, in the corner of a concrete yard, sitting all alone, was a little West Highland White Terrier.

I dashed back to reception and, breathless, I enquired about it.

'Her name is Toller and she's a five-year-old pedigree bitch. She has just been dropped off and the vet hasn't even seen her yet. We know nothing about her,' the girl remarked.

'I would like to have her,' I stated.

She looked startled. 'There is a waiting list, and we don't know whether she's suitable for re-homing yet. But you can fill in an application form.'

I filled in the paper work and asked when I could have her.

'Phone in a week and we'll let you know what the vet says,' was all she would say.

Little White Pet

A week later I phoned up.

'Her hair's been cut, and a chip has been put in her. The vet is treating her for itchy skin, but she's a lovely temperament.'

'When can I pick her up?' I asked.

'Come and visit her in a week and we'll discuss it.'

The following Saturday I said to Susy, 'We're going out and would like you to come for the trip, too.' Her curiosity was aroused and she wanted to know where we were going.

'It's a surprise,' is all I would say.

When we arrived, she was full of excitement. I handed her a leaflet and it mentioned that if you adopt one of their animals you can visit them regularly.

'Can we do that?' she asked eagerly.

'We'll see,' I said, as noncommittal as I could be.

I went to reception and told the girl we had come to get Toller. The girl brought the dog to us on a lead. She immediately jumped up on Susy and licked her all over as if she was a long-lost friend. Susy was totally captivated.

'Can we have her?' she pleaded.

'Yes,' I answered her. 'We can take her home when she's ready.'

The girl explained that the vet was still treating her itchy skin and she couldn't leave for a week.

'We'll be back in a week and will take her home

then,' I told the girl. So it was all agreed and the appropriate arrangements were made.

It was the longest week of Susy's life. Each day seemed like a month and the week was a lifetime. However, the Saturday eventually arrived and we set off to fetch Toller. We bought a bed, a lead and some food and put her in the back of the car with Susy. She walked into our house with her tail wagging and was happy from the start. She was gentle and sweet-natured, never retaliating whatever happened to her. We could even take a biscuit out of her mouth without her minding. Apart from her itchy skin, she also suffered from stress incontinence at the beginning. If a man lifted a hand to stroke her, she would immediately produce a puddle and cower with fright. I can only imagine she must have been hit at her previous home. Her other fear was of bangs – thunder or fireworks. If there was a thunder storm she would run upstairs and dive under our bed, shaking with fear. It was the only time I allowed her to go up. One dark October evening, she wanted to go out into the garden and I opened the door for her. All of a sudden there was a big bang as someone let off a firework. She shot around the house and into the road, disappearing round the corner. Henry leapt into the car and I ran after her down the lane. We searched everywhere we could in Chard, up and down each road, calling and looking round every turning. Nothing. We were devastated. We returned home with our hearts in our boots. As we arrived home the phone rang.

'Hello,' the voice said. 'Have you lost a little white dog?'

It was the stationers in the centre of Chard. They were still open and Toller had seen the lights on in the shop and had wandered in. I would hate to think how many roads she had crossed in the process. We fetched her and she was none the worse for her ordeal.

Toller began to struggle with her health when she reached twelve years of age. I took her to the vet.

'I'm afraid it's bad news,' he said. 'She has a large tumour on her spleen and I can't operate.'

This was terrible news. I took her home and discussed the situation with Henry and with Susy, who was by then living in Bristol.

'Don't do anything before the weekend,' she pleaded. 'I'm coming down to say goodbye.'

It was a very sad weekend, and Monday came all too quickly. Henry and I both took her to the vet who had agreed to put her down. I cuddled her in my arms, and as her body went limp, I wept uncontrollably. But it was a peaceful end to a friend who had given us all so much joy. We scattered her ashes on our garden, then looked for a rose bush to plant on top. As we studied the names, we came across one called 'Little White Pet.' That had to be the one. We planted it in full view of our windows and it blossoms abundantly every year.

Chapter Ten

A Sinking Feeling

We waved goodbye to Pete as he got into James' car for the journey to Heathrow Airport with my heart in my boots. He was eighteen and just starting off on the biggest adventure of his life to sail across the South China Sea.

'It will be alright mum. Don't worry,' he called to me. This was what he always said to me but I couldn't help worrying and I said a heartfelt prayer, 'Please God look after him. I can't anymore, so it's over to You now.'

His love of sailing started way back when he was in year eight at Holyrood School. His science teacher, Dick Pavey, arranged for any children who wanted to learn to sail to go to Durleigh Reservoir, near Bridgewater, every Tuesday after school, throughout the summer terms. Pete took to it like a duck to water and became very proficient. He later joined Lyme Regis Sailing Club and taught sailing to the younger ones.

In 1998 he had the opportunity to join the Ocean

Youth Club and sail on the first leg of the Cutty Sark Tall Ships race from Falmouth to Lisbon. He would be sailing on the 'Team Spirit of Wight', the OYC flagship, with twenty-two other young people, of whom fifteen would be inexperienced trainees, and seven were qualified. They would be racing against about a hundred other ships, including Mir, one of the fastest of the large ships in the world and a truly massive Russian beast. Pete was so excited. He was taken down to Falmouth by minibus on July the thirteenth, in order to give the crew a chance to accustom themselves to their ketch.

Henry and I drove down to Falmouth on the sixteenth. We left at six o'clock in the morning in order to avoid the Saturday traffic, and arrived at the car park before it had opened. It was a beautiful, sunny day with a warm breeze, ideal weather conditions for the race, and we wandered around until we were allowed to go near to the 'Team Spirit of Wight' and call across to Pete. When I saw the size of the boat, I was shocked.

'Look how tiny it is compared with the other ships," I pointed out to Henry. "Surely they will never be safe when battling against the wind and the waves at sea, especially in the Bay of Biscay.' I breathed another prayer.

The ships began leaving one by one at around nine o'clock and there was a carnival atmosphere.

Multicoloured flags flapped, sightseers jostled for position, and there was a Cornish Pasty crisis; Falmouth had already sold out, though I understand that later the fish out in the Atlantic Ocean were well-fed on the digested remains of them! We hurried up the hill to the top of the headland in order to watch the Parade of Sail out in the Falmouth Bay. They were an impressive sight, all one hundred ships in full sail, and we watched in amazement as the huge Mir sailed passed us, with the crew all standing to attention on the spars, saluting as they stood there in their smart uniforms. It was a sight to behold. There were many spectacular boats, but the one we were straining to see was Team Spirit of Wight.

'There it is,' we chorused. It looked like a toy boat among the monsters of the sea.

Watching on the sidelines was the cruise liner, QE2, and she looked impressive as she gleamed white in the bright morning sun, booming out her greeting to them on her horns as they sailed out of sight.

It took them about ten days to reach Lisbon. They were not first in their class, but no one cared and they had all had a whale of a time. They spent a week in Lisbon where a huge international party had been organised for them, with young people from every nation you could think of. Pete arrived back at Heathrow in the early hours of August the third, tired but happy.

He worked for the local meat factory that winter, but come Easter of the following year he was off crewing again for the Ocean Youth Trust (as it had been renamed), mainly to France and the Channel Islands. He was then offered the chance to become boson on the Spirit of Boadicea. He jumped at the opportunity and travelled with the ship to Belgium, Holland and up and down the canals, carrying on board several cargoes of teenage boys who were on probation. On one trip, when they were due to return, a gale force eight wind blew up. Pete related the story.

'We dropped off the boys so that they could take the ferry back to England as it was too rough for them to stay on board,' he explained. 'But Skipper, first mate and I had to bring the boat back, sailing across the North Sea. It took us twenty-four hours, battling against the wind and waves, which were twenty feet high at times. We had to take it in turns to steer our little boat, and we were strapped onto the rail so we wouldn't be swept overboard as the waves lashed against us. I found it exhilarating and exciting and wasn't a bit scared.'

That winter he was back at the meat factory, but once spring poked its nose around the corner, Pete's call of the sea raised its head again. He decided to join Crewseekers, an internet site for those looking for crewing jobs. It was not until Monday, the twenty fourth of April that he saw the job he wanted. He applied and got an email reply:

"*The boat is a Tayana 43, Taiwan built, strong and good cruiser, full safety equipment and ready to sail. Crew are me and Christian, both 31, both Italians, 50,000 nm experience in every oceans. The delivery cover 2500 nm approx, will stop in Singapore, Langkawi and Phuket.....We should leave first days of may, say 1,2,3 so we need a crew arriving at least the 1st of may. Cheers Cese e Christian.*"

The rest of the note was about money – or the lack of it – but Pete immediately replied to Cese and was offered the job. On Tuesday he gave in his notice at work. On Wednesday he bought a single ticket to Hong Kong. On Thursday he had his inoculations at the surgery. On Friday he packed his case and on Saturday he was gone. We did not have time to prepare ourselves.

The house seemed eerily empty when Pete was away, and this time was no exception. We looked at the map to follow the route he would take and imagined the adventure he was having.

Three weeks later, the telephone rang .

'Hi, mum. Pete here.'

I was really surprised to hear him. Surely they could not have reached land so soon.

'How lovely to hear you. Where are you?'

'In Bangkok. The boat sank,' he announced. As I gasped, he continued. 'But it's alright. We were rescued and we're quite safe now. We're at the home of the boat's owner. He's the managing director of a large firm and he lives in a luxury complex, along side ambassadors and other rich people. We have servants to look after us, armed guards to protect us and a huge car driven by a chauffeur to take us around Bangkok. At the moment I'm lying beside the swimming pool in the sun, drinking a glass of bubbly. I've got to go, bye.' And with that, he was gone. I was speechless.

It wasn't until the end of the summer that he returned home and filled us in with the details of what had happened. We sat down together and he told us his story.

'I was met at Hong Kong airport on the Sunday by Cese and Christian and we set sail on the Monday. The first ten days were wonderful; hot, sunny and relaxing as we gently cruised our way across the South China Sea. Then disaster struck. All the electrics failed. It was a modern boat and everything on it was controlled by the electrical supply – including raising the sails, steering and lighting. We tried everything to mend it, but couldn't. We were drifting helplessly in the sea, with no way of avoiding the big ships that would be unable to see us in the dark. We started to feel alarmed. We drifted into a patch of seaweed and the rudder got caught up in it. Cese asked me if I would dive in and disentangle the rudder. I did try but I couldn't hold my breath for long enough to do it and came back up. It was only later they told me that the sea was shark-infested. Probably just as well.'

'Was the sea rough?' Henry asked.

'It was becoming choppy as the sun was beginning to set. We sent out a mayday message, asking for assistance. No one responded. There were a lot of pirates about in those waters and all the ships were giving us a wide berth for fear it was a trap. The day was rapidly passing by and we were desperate. Eventually we received a response from the crew of a great cargo ship, called the Ambrosia, which was unable to stop, but the crew said they would throw us a line as they drew near. We were so relieved and we waited eagerly as the ship came nearer. It was massive, about quarter of a mile long, and towered above us. Cese was looking very anxious and he explained why. He told me to look at the size of the propeller. It was sucking into it everything that floated on the water, and chewing it into little pieces before spitting it out. We would not stand a chance if we went anywhere near it. The crew threw the rope to us but it fell into the water. They pulled it back up and had another attempt. We were afraid they would miss again and we might not get another chance as the ship was moving rapidly and we were drifting towards its propeller. We had run out of options. Fortunately, Cese managed to catch the rope and he tied it securely to Tayana, which wasn't easy as she was bobbing frantically about in the surging wake of the ship.'

He paused here, as the horror of the situation came flooding back to him.

'The ship had a lift which descended down its side. A couple of the crew came down on it but our little boat was being tossed about like a cork and they couldn't reach us. Cese told me to leave my bag behind. I would need both hands if I was going to get onto the lift safely. I was determined, though, to take it and flung it over my shoulder. I had to time my leap to coincide with being level with them. I waited. Another wave was coming and as it tossed us up in the air, I jumped. I felt two pairs of strong arms clutch hold of me and pull me onto their platform. I could feel the perspiration on my face, mingled with the salty spray. My knees felt weak with the effort, and I stood trembling as Cese and Christian made the same manoeuvre. Gradually the lift began to rise up the side of the ship and eventually we reached the deck and were helped on board by the crew.

The Tayana was being towed along, bobbing up

and down in the swell beside us. In the morning we looked over the rail for it and found, to our horror, it was gone. The rope had broken and it had sunk into the deep waters with all our possessions, including all my CDs. We were very upset, but I was pleased I had brought my bag with me!'

Pete laughed, and we had to agree with him that it was fortunate he still had his bag of clothes.

'We sailed for a week and the crew made us very welcome, although no-one spoke English. When the ship docked at Da Nang, we said goodbye to the crew, thanked them a thousand times for rescuing us, then the three of us went by train to Bangkok. That was where the owner of the fated Tayana lived, and he met us at the station and took us to his home. He told us not to worry about the loss of the boat as he was fully insured.'

I began to tremble with the horror of his story and I gave thanks to God for looking after him and keeping him safe.

The life of luxury lasted a week before Pete was put on a plane and flown back to Hong Kong.

'There I was contracted to look after, and do maintenance work on, a sixty-three-foot ketch sitting in Hong Kong harbour. But I was lonely, and my little flat was on the other side of Hong Kong. I knew no-one and couldn't speak Chinese so decided to quit. I phoned up Cese. He and Christian were running sailing trips around the Canary Islands so I flew off to join them. It was definitely an improvement on my previous job! It came to an end after two weeks and they returned to Italy, but I went to Spain and travelled by train to Gibraltar in the hope of getting some work on a boat with an English speaking crew. I was unable to find any, but I did meet up with two British lads who were on their way to backpack across Africa. I was definitely up for this challenge and joined them and their tent as they crossed over to Morocco. I was fascinated by the different scenery and way of life as we travelled along and really enjoyed it.'

My mind went back to that trip. Pete was pretty good at keeping in touch, either by short phone calls, or else by emails sent from cyber cafes, but his next email was from Marrakesh. My heart had sunk when I'd read it. It said that he had run out of money. He could not afford to buy any food or clean water. He was sleeping rough. Of course he had not taken any malaria drugs or other inoculations before he went there and was very vulnerable to the worst that Africa had to throw at him. As another prayer went up to God I had emailed back. 'Go back to Europe. At least they have clean (comparatively) water and a good health service.' For once in his life, Pete had responded to my plea and the three of them returned to Spain.

He continued with his story. 'Once we were back in Spain we decided to take a boat to Ibiza. I borrowed money from my friends and survived that way. While in Ibiza, I made a wonderful discovery – there was a lot of money to be made from seasonal work, once the English tourists arrived, doing promotional work for the bars and clubs. I was pretty good at selling tickets and doing their promotions so got a lot of work. But it all finished at the end of summer, once the Brits. had gone home. So here I am, back in Chard, still in one piece.'

I am so grateful to God for taking care of him throughout his adventures.

Chapter Eleven

The 'C' Word

I walked nervously up the steps of the breast screening van to the waiting receptionist. It was my lunch time at the social services' office where I worked as a community occupational therapist and I could think of many things I would rather do than come here. I came regularly every few years, so knew what to expect. I was not looking forward to it.

The receptionist took my details and told me to wait until I was called. I fidgeted as I sat down with a Reader's Digest in my hands. I would go to the jokes... that should distract me. They did not seem that funny as I glanced through them. My name was called and I went into a cubicle to change. It was so small I wondered how a large lady would manage. I undressed my top half and slipped my cardigan back on. I went into the room where the radiographer held the instrument of torture in her hands. She was very pleasant and asked me to place my breast on the plate. As she compressed it and twisted it I wondered how I would have reacted if I'd been one of the early Christian martyrs being persecuted for my faith. Would I have given in easily and agreed to anything I was told? Possibly so. I was brought back sharply by her gentle voice asking me to do the same with my other breast. The whole thing was over in minutes and I was soon dressed and walking back into the sunshine, relieved to know that it would be some years before I had to go through it again.

A couple of weeks later a letter was posted through our letterbox. It was an official looking one from Taunton Hospital. It would be my all-clear following my mammogram, I surmised. I opened it and stared in horror. It was from the oncology department, asking me to come for another mammogram. Oncology meant cancer. Why did they want to see me again? Surely they had not found anything. The appointment was only a few days away, for which I was thankful. In the morning I called pastor Neil Reid. I asked if I could come and see him. He was waiting for me when Henry and I turned up in his office. I explained the situation and he prayed for me straight away, that I should be healed in the name of Jesus.

I arrived at the oncology reception desk feeling confident. I did not have to wait long. When I walked in, the radiographer had my X-ray pinned on the wall with a light behind. It showed a picture of my breast.

What a Coincidence!

And there in the middle was a clear, white blob, about a centimetre across. My heart froze. She did not have to say anything. It leapt off the screen and shouted cancer at me. I wanted to cry. I was too young to die. I wasn't even sixty. And what about my family? How could I tell them? Even my parents were still alive. I wanted to celebrate my father's hundredth birthday with him. I could not die before my mum and dad. I was jolted back into the present.

'Take off your upper garments and then come over here, please,' the girl requested.

I did as I was told, feeling quite numb. She put me in the mammogram machine and took the pictures.

'Wait over there while I look at them,' she said.

I took a seat and waited. It seemed like hours before she returned, but my watch said it was only a few minutes.

'I'm sorry, but I can't find it. I'll have to take the pictures again.'

At that moment, I knew it had gone. I smiled broadly.

'No problem,' I said.

I hardly noticed any discomfort, I was so elated. She returned with my x-rays and told me she could find no lump on any of them so she would like the doctor to examine me.

I went into another room where there was a bed

and was asked to lie on it. The doctor prodded and poked and squeezed first one breast, then the other.

Eventually she said, 'I would like a second opinion. I am going to ask another doctor to examine you.'

The second doctor was just as thorough, but came to the same conclusion. There was nothing there. I was free to go.

Henry and I had a great celebration that night.

Chapter Twelve

Muscle-Wasting Disease

'You ought to go to the doctor and ask him if you should have a hip replacement,' I urged Henry one day when he was limping badly.

He had had some difficulty walking for a few years, but was reluctant to bother his G.P. about it while he could manage. He agreed and made an appointment.

'It isn't a hip problem,' announced the doctor, after examining him thoroughly. 'I'm going to refer you to the Neurologist at Musgrove Hospital.'

It was some months before Henry was eventually given an appointment to see the consultant neurologist. We drove along the country route to Taunton, admiring the mats of aubretia and golden alyssum along the way, and the ancient stone walls spangled with pink and white cotoneaster. The scenery lifted both our spirits and we arrived at Musgrove hospital in a good mood.

We did not have to wait long before seeing the

consultant. He examined all Henry's muscles very closely. He laid him on the examination bed and looked at his arms first. He asked Henry to move them this way and that. Then he asked him to push his arms against his own. He wrote his detailed findings down in Henry's notes. Next he looked at his legs. He commented on the wasting muscles on his thighs. He got him to push his legs against his hands. Again he wrote it all down in the notes. I sat there without a word, wondering what it all meant.

Eventually he spoke.

'You have a muscle-wasting disease called Body Inclusion Myositis,' he said to Henry.

'It is degenerative and has no cure,' he added.

We were both completely shocked by this announcement. It was so unexpected.

'Will Henry end up in a wheelchair?' we asked, not wanting to hear the answer.

He told us that he would, but not for a while. He explained that although the disease was progressive, it was usually slow. Keeping Henry's weight down would help. This was not what Henry, who was a great lover of chocolate cake, wanted to hear! He said he would like to do a biopsy, but as he could do nothing to halt the course of the disease, we could see no point.

We did not accept that this was God's will for Henry's life, and after prayer, he just got on with life. We noticed no deterioration in his condition, and we

What a Coincidence!

kept on walking and enjoying ourselves as we had before.

Eighteen months later, the neurologist sent a letter and asked to see Henry again. We made the appointment and attended his clinic. It seemed ages that we were sat in the waiting room, and I browsed through the magazines laid out beside us. There was an article about Amy Winehouse and her antics. Also Tom Jones, who was strutting his stuff again. I put the magazine down and did a bit of people-watching, imagining what had happened to all these people in the waiting room to bring them here. Then it was our turn.

We walked in and sat down. The neurologist asked Henry to stand up. The first thing he commented on was the fact that Henry had stood up without using the arms of the chair to help him. He then examined all Henry's muscles as he had before, laying him on the examination bed and studying one limb at a time. As before, he wrote in Henry's notes as he went along. We awaited his verdict with bated breath.

'I can find nothing wrong with you,' he eventually announced, with great surprise. 'All your limbs seem perfectly normal to me.'

He had no explanation.

'I don't need to see you again,' he assured Henry. 'You're fine.'

Muscle-Wasting Disease

We dove home that day with our hearts singing. Our gratitude to God knew no bounds.

Recently, Henry had to go into Musgrove Hospital to have a pacemaker fitted for an irregular heartbeat. He was awake during the operation so that the surgeon could ask him to cough at certain moments, though he had plenty of local anaesthetic so that he felt no pain. The surgeon started cutting through the muscle in Henry's left shoulder.

He asked, 'How old are you?' Henry replied that he was seventy-one.

The surgeon said, 'Well, you have the muscles of a much younger man. Your muscles are hard and difficult to cut, unlike the soft tissue I would expect at seventy-one!'

Had God not only healed his diseased muscles, but replaced them with new, young ones?

Chapter Thirteen

What Happened to July?

'Stand back!' shouted the paramedic.

Henry's body jumped as she applied the defibrillator to his chest. There was still no pulse.

With one last desperate attempt, she called again, 'Stand back!'

This time she detected a faint pulse and so she and her colleague lifted Henry off the floor and onto the stretcher, before moving him into the ambulance.

It was the twenty-eighth of June, 2009 and the day had started well enough. Henry had driven me to South Chard Church half an hour before the start of the eleven o'clock Sunday service so that we would have plenty of time to talk to people. The band had already arrived in order to do the sound check, which AJ Dunster was about to organise. Others were milling around getting things ready.

As Henry walked in, he felt a little giddy and sat down. That was the last thing he remembered. He collapsed on the chair. He was not breathing and he had no pulse. Mikey Powell, our tall and lanky worship leader who was eighteen years old, was just walking up to the stage. He hurriedly came back and dialled 999. The person on the other end of the phone told the people around Henry to lay him on the floor and start CPR. AJ used to be a lifeguard and knew what to do. He pounded Henry's heart with vigour. He was a strong man, used to physical work at the abattoir, but he began to tire after a while. Others took turns. Where was the ambulance? Even the paramedic's car or first responder had not arrived. Twenty minutes went by. It seemed like a lifetime and Henry was showing no signs of life. I stood watching, sobbing uncontrollably, as his eyes stared lifelessly ahead, seeing nothing. He looked so dead. Charmaine, AJ's wife, put a comforting arm round me and insisted that I drank the cup of sweet tea I had been brought.

'It is good for shock,' she explained, 'You need to drink it.'

The ambulance eventually arrived and two paramedics walked into the church. They saw at once the situation and fetched their defibrillator. They gave him two shocks and managed to feel a pulse. They transferred him into the ambulance and got him wired up. People had started arriving at the church car park while all this was going on. Neil, our pastor, asked them to go into the centre, behind the church. He would call them when it was all clear, though he wondered how he was going to take the service after this.

I phoned James in Cheltenham. The first time there was no reply. I tried again. This time he answered. He told me that he had ignored his phone the first time as he was busy. The second time he had looked to see who it was. He saw it was me. He wondered why I was not in church at eleven o'clock. Suddenly the penny dropped; it must be dad. I talked to him between sobs and told him what had happened.

'I'll be with you in a couple of hours,' he assured me.

An air ambulance had been called and it had to land at the top of the field opposite the church until the farmer could move his cows and bull out of the way and he could land nearer. The ambulance drove down the road to the far gate, then realised the helicopter had moved and reversed all the way back. I was in the car driven by Luke Talmage, our associate pastor, with Sue, AJ's mum, beside me for support. We followed the ambulance down the road, then had to reverse quickly as it sped back towards us. A great crowd of onlookers had arrived by now. It was not often a helicopter landed in the little village of South Chard! The electric fence was taken down and Henry was transferred into the helicopter where he was flown to Musgrove. On his way there Henry suffered another cardiac arrest but again the paramedics managed to resuscitate him.

In A&E he was put in the resuscitation room, where a team of doctors and nurses tried to stabilise him. By now, Luke and Sue had reached the hospital with me. Susy, our daughter, was at Kelly's hen-party in Chard. She was a school friend and Susy was to be chief bridesmaid at her wedding, so they were all having a sleepover. I rang Susy in tears and they rushed her to the hospital. Her boyfriend, Tom, soon arrived from Bristol. James and his girlfriend, Fiona, were on their way. Pete was some way behind them as he had to drive all the way from Leeds.

Henry, who was in the recovery room in A&E, was very noisy and thrashed about. They told me that it was cerebral disturbance. We were put in the family room, away from the crowded waiting room. The cardiac nurse was very kind and came to see us frequently to let us know what was happening.

'As he has been without a pulse for twenty minutes he will have suffered extensive brain damage,' she explained. 'If he does recover, he won't recognise you, I'm afraid.'

We were allowed to go in to see him, but he was completely unconscious and there was a lot of activity around his bed. Eventually he was stabilised and we were told that he would be taken up to the intensive care unit (ICU). We decided to go to the restaurant for a sandwich and then went up to ICU to see him. We were told to wait in the visitors' room while they settled him in. We waited and we waited. Eventually James and Fiona wandered off to see what was happening. They could get no response. After a couple of hours we were eventually allowed in. We went in two at a time. He lay there unconscious, wired up to their machines and drips.

'He will be very brain damaged if he ever comes round,' the ICU nurse warned us. 'I have put him on a ventilator to help him breathe and have sedated him so that he will be in an induced coma for twenty-four hours. He won't wake up before then.'

We had a family discussion. We might as well all go out and get something to eat. We would need to keep our strength up and there were obviously going to be no more developments today.

It was just after six-thirty in the evening as we all walked past his room. It was the only room visible from the corridor. The nurse saw us as we all filed past and she called to us, so James and I went in. Henry was just beginning to stir! (Later I found out that this had been the time the church were praying for him, at the start of the evening service.) He recognised us straight away and wanted to know what had happened. We filled him in with the details.

'What!' he exclaimed. 'I've had a ride in a helicopter, and didn't know anything about it! Did anyone have a camera and take photos?' he enquired.

We had to admit that finding a camera wasn't the first thing on our minds! Much to his disappointment I didn't even remember what colour the helicopter was. He was very pleased to see all the family, but he was amazed he had missed a whole day with us. As he was now obviously alright, we were told that he would be taken into the Cardiac Care Unit. We all went off for our meal with light hearts.

The next day they started all the tests to find out what had happened. The MRI scan revealed nothing, the angiogram showed his arteries were fine and the blood tests all came back negative. On the Thursday morning I prayed that God would show them the problem. When I went in to see him that morning, the nurse met me.

'Henry had another episode this morning,' she explained to me. 'There is nothing to worry about. We were able to deal with it straight away before he could have another cardiac arrest. The good news is that we now have a read-out of his problem. His heart started racing so the consultant will be round to see you both soon to explain what he can do about it.'

The surgeon came to see us later that morning.

'This problem can easily be solved,' he began. 'We

need to take out your pacemaker and replace it by an ICD (Internal Cardioverter Defibrillator). This piece of equipment,' he continued, 'will pace your heart if it goes too slowly or too quickly, but will also give you an electric shock if your heart stops. It will cost £15, 000 and I will have to apply for funding to the Hospital Trust.

As I drove home that night I was very aware of the lovely countryside around me. Already some of the cornfields looked ready for cutting, and the Queen Anne's lace, which had enhanced the green verges, had been replaced by scabious and knapweed. We lived in such a beautiful part of the world.

Funding was granted for the ICD and Henry had the operation on the ninth of July. He had to be awake for it and it was painful at times.

As his Warfrin had to be stopped for the operation, he was put on Heparin, which is a faster acting blood thinner. This proved too much for his system and he had internal bleeding, making his scar site swell up. The surgeon was worried.

'I can't leave it like that,' he explained. 'I'll ask the nurses to put a pressure pad on to see if they can diffuse the swelling.'

The nurses applied a pressure pad, which was quite uncomfortable, but it had no effect. Henry was taken back to theatre five days later and the surgeon cleaned it all up, mopped up the blood and sealed it with hydrogen peroxide.

The next day he developed an infection in the wound and it became swollen and weepy. He was on intravenous antibiotics and everyone hoped that they would be effective. The nurses dressed it daily all that week, willing it to clear up.

At lunch time I took a walk around the hospital grounds. I needed some fresh air. It was all so worrying and I did not know what to think. I sat on one of the seats in the sunshine and watched a family of swallows. Their first brood were already accomplished fliers and the parents were busy building a second nest under the hospital eaves. I wondered what had made them reject their first home. It was a lot of extra work for them.

On the next Monday the surgeon came to see Henry. After studying the notes and examining the wound, he gave his verdict.

'It will all have to come out,' he told us. 'You will need a new ICD put in on the other side of your chest, and the old site will have to be sewn back up. Taking the old one out will be tricky, as the wires have to be removed from your heart and that can cause bleeding. I can't do that as I have no cardiac thoracic team to support me if that should happen. I will send you to Bristol and you can have the operation there.'

This was disastrous news. We were going to have to

start again from the beginning. It would mean another long wait before anything would be done and the Bristol Royal Infirmary would be so inconvenient for visitors. It seemed like the last straw after all Henry had been through. We held hands and cried.

We decided to send for Pastor Neil to come and pray for Henry that evening and anoint him with oil. God was now the only One who could help us. Neil arrived within the hour and was able to pray for us both and encourage us.

The next morning the surgeon came to see Henry again and told him he had passed him on to Bristol for them to deal with him.

'I would like you to do the operation,' said Henry. 'I am confident that everything will be alright. I am willing to take the risk.'

The surgeon was reluctant but then he changed his mind and agreed to do it the next day.

On the twenty-second of July, he took everything out of the left side of Henry's chest and wired a new ICD into the right side. This took over four hours and, although he was awake, he felt nothing. Everything went very well and the surgeon was really pleased with it all. The scar had no swelling, no infection and even no bruising. They were going to put him back on Heparin, but his INR (International Normalised Ratio, used to measure the clotting tendency of blood) went up so fast with the Warfrin that they did not need to. They kept him on intravenous antibiotics for a week, then discharged him. It had been a long journey, but everything had worked out well in the end.

I had a lot to celebrate, not just his complete recovery, but also the engagement of James and Fiona. And for Christmas, the children clubbed together and bought us a ride on a helicopter.

Chapter Fourteen

Larger than Life

I viewed the leg apprehensively. Henry's left leg had begun to swell.

'It's probably this hot weather,' he said, sounding more nonchalant than he felt.

The year of 2010 had produced a very hot June, it was true, but for it to cause only one leg to swell seemed unlikely.

'Have you been taking your water tablets regularly?' I enquired.

'Of course,' he retorted, then added, 'when we aren't going out!'

We decided to ignore it. It was bound to go down eventually. But it never did; in fact it continued to swell.

Three weeks later, on July the fourteenth, Henry woke up and tried to climb out of bed.

'My leg is ever so stiff,' he complained. 'I can't bend it.'

He took off his pyjamas and we stared at it. It was

like a balloon with the skin so tight that his knee would not bend. Added to that, a bruise had appeared on his inside thigh, spreading upwards towards his hip.

'I think you'd better see the doctor.' I tried not to let my voice sound worried. 'I'm going to the ladies' meeting at church. I'll ask them to pray.'

Henry waited for his number to come up on the screen in the surgery. It was a very modern system and patients were expected to book themselves in on a computer when they entered the waiting room. This resulted in a slip of paper being spat out of the machine like a parking ticket. It had a number on it, and you had to sit among the rows of coughs and colds until your number flashed up on the screen. Henry's number eventually appeared and he limped up the corridor to the doctor's room, leaning heavily on his stick. The doctor was standing at the door waiting for him, and as Henry had his shorts on that morning, made an instant exclamation about his leg. He examined him thoroughly and felt the swollen area under his knee.

'It could be a Baker's cyst,' he explained, 'but you need to go to hospital straight away to have it examined properly. They'll do an ultrasound scan and be able to diagnose it accurately.'

He phoned Musgrove Hospital and told Henry to go to ward two, where they would arrange the scan.

We set off under a bright blue sky and decided to drive the back route to Taunton via Neroche Forest. The hedgerows were at their most lush and the trees showed off in their competition to be the greenest, displaying every shade possible. The lambs were almost adult size but still young enough to cavort about, butting each other and their long-suffering mothers. The sun shone brightly through the trees, and the light flashed on and off like neon lighting.

I dropped Henry off at the entrance of the hospital while I went to park. When I arrived, I chased after him and then realised how long the distance was that he was expected to walk along the corridors. It must have been over quarter of a mile to the ward and I expected to see him lying down in the corridor, suffering from exhaustion. However, a kindly porter had taken pity on him and wheeled him to his bed!

After the initial interrogation by the nurse, we eventually saw a doctor. She examined his leg carefully and explained what the problem was.

'It's a popliteal aneurysm,' she stated. 'We will put you on the emergency operation list for Friday afternoon.'

She drew a little diagram to illustrate the operation, then added: 'We'll have to bypass the aneurysm and attach a plastic blood vessel in its place. Tomorrow you will have an ultrasound scan to pinpoint its position.'

'Does that mean I have to stay in?' asked Henry.

'Oh, yes,' she replied. 'You will be in for some while as we have to stop your Warfarin before the operation and start it again afterwards. You won't be going anywhere until your INR (international normalised ratio) is at a good level.'

We were both shocked. This was supposed to be an afternoon visit to have a scan. Oh well, I would have to go home and pack his bag once more.

The next morning was another beautiful day. What a shame to be wasting it inside a hot, germy hospital. I arrived after lunch as morning visiting was not allowed on the ward. Henry had not returned from having his ultrasound scan so I started chatting to a man in a neighbouring bed. He was an amputee, and moved his wheelchair towards me.

'What did you come in for?' I asked.

'Well I came in with a swollen leg like Henry's and they chopped it off,' he explained.

That was not what I wanted to hear and my heart sank into my boots. I changed the subject quickly. I certainly did not want to hear any more about his leg!

Eventually Henry returned.

'She spent ages scanning my leg from every angle,' he told me. 'I shall be interested to hear the results.'

It was a long afternoon waiting to see a doctor. I whiled away the time doing Sudoku puzzles and Henry enjoyed the finer points of his *Buses Magazine*. It was sometime before a doctor arrived. She seemed very surprised by the scan.

'We can't find anything on it at all,' she announced. 'We'll send you for an MRI scan tomorrow morning and see what that shows up.'

'I can't go in the big tube,' Henry replied. 'I have an ICD (Implantable Cardioverter Defibrillator) fitted inside my chest.'

She hadn't noticed. 'We'll just do your legs,' she agreed and added the instructions to his notes.

'It's just as well I wasn't unconscious or demented or I would have been in trouble,' Henry grumbled to me later. 'You would have thought she might have read my notes first!'

When I turned up the next afternoon, Henry had been for his MRI scan and was waiting to go down for an X-ray. The porter soon arrived and whisked him away. He was gone for most of the afternoon as they could not find a porter to bring him back. Time seems to stand still in hospitals. We had another long wait for the doctor to appear. This time it was the registrar.

'I am perplexed,' he said, as he examined Henry's leg. 'All the tests have shown up nothing at all. I have no idea what the problem is. We'll send you for another ultrasound scan tomorrow, on a different machine, just to make sure we haven't missed anything.'

The next morning Henry was taken for another scan. When I arrived in the afternoon the doctor was with him.

'Nothing has shown up again, and his leg is looking less swollen, so he might as well go home and see what happens. Go back to your GP if you are worried about it.'

We returned home, enjoying the glorious sunshine as we drove back through Neroche Forest, and rejoicing that God had got to his leg before the doctors did!

Chapter Fifteen

A Shoulder Story

The phone rang. It was my sister, Enid. It was always a joy to hear her voice. Usually she phoned from her bath on a Saturday morning, but this was an evening in the week. I knew she would be tired after spending all day on her feet as a vascular technologist at Bristol Royal Infirmary.

'How are you enjoying this Arctic weather?' I asked.

It was November, 2010 and the temperatures had dropped to minus eleven degrees centigrade in Chard, and even colder in some places. Everywhere was covered in a blanket of snow and the country had almost come to a standstill with airports closed, motorways impassible and trains at a standstill. I had never known winter arrive so early. It had become a nightmare for those who had to travel, but for those of us who could stay indoors and look at it, it was like a Christmas card. The heavy hoar frost made the trees look like beautiful, artistic creations, and the virgin snow dazzled orange in the glow of the setting sun.

A Shoulder Story

'I'm ringing to ask you to pray,' she said. 'Joy has fallen down and has broken her shoulder.'

'I'm so sorry,' I replied. 'Of course I'll pray. That must be so painful. Can they do anything for her?'

'She has it in a sling and has to keep it still,' she commented. 'But that isn't the problem.' There was a pause and I heard her taking a breath. 'When she had the x-ray on her shoulder, they found something else. A 'mass' of some sort has shown up in the neck area. They don't know at this point whether it is malignant or not so they are going to do a biopsy on it.'

I was devastated. Not our lovely Joy! She was only twenty eight and so full of life. I thought of her beautiful, dark hair which fell in thick waves down her back. I wondered what she would look like, after chemotherapy, if she lost it all. It was unthinkable.

'Of course I'll pray,' I exclaimed. 'It's the ladies' meeting tomorrow morning so I'll ask them to pray with me.'

I was anxious to know what was happening, so I e-mailed Joy and asked to hear her story. She told me all about it.

'I was coming home one night in November and it was very cold. Within sight of my front door I decided to make a run for it. Somehow my foot got caught and I launched myself into a parked car before smacking down onto the ground.

'I was unable to move, partly because of the shock and partly because of the pain. Luckily, Chris, my boyfriend, was there and came rushing over to see if I was ok. My right shoulder and left knee were really painful and the situation wasn't improved by him grabbing my arm to try and lift me off the ground! I eventually made it to my feet and went to bed feeling pretty sore and silly.

'When I woke up in the morning, the pain had intensified. I knew it was more than scrapes and bruises. We went to A&E on the Sunday and were told the wait was five-and-a-half hours. I turned to Chris and suggested we go and get some lunch and come back later. He told me in no uncertain terms we'd be staying until we'd been seen by the doctor!

'The X-rays showed I had fractured my greater tuberosity (a bone in my shoulder). They put me in a sling and told me to keep it as still as possible. That first day was agony; I had to stop walking after every few steps as searing pain shot through my arm.

'A week later I went back to fracture clinic to have it X-rayed again. The X-ray showed the bone had started to heal. However, on mentioning that I also had pain in my neck and some trouble swallowing, the doctor told me to get that X-rayed too.

'This X-ray showed no breaks or fractures, but the doctor suggested I see my GP about the swallowing problem. With other things uppermost on my mind, I shoved this to the bottom of my to-do list and carried on with my slow left-handed typing and other such amusing activities.

'Ten days or so later I went back to fracture clinic. They gave me some exercises to do to get my shoulder moving and seemed happy with my progress. Then the doctor asked me if I'd seen my GP about the swallowing problem. I admitted that I hadn't. Looking rather grave he persuaded me to do so.

"Without meaning to sound sinister," he said, "you need to get that looked at. The radiographers saw some excess tissue in your throat and it needs to be checked out."

'I realised the situation was a little more pressing than I had thought and made an appointment with my doctor for the next day.

'When I saw my GP I explained what the hospital doctor had said and he felt my throat. I immediately felt he was about to fob me off.

"I don't know what I'm supposed to do if I can't see the X-rays and I've got nothing else to go on," he said.

'But then two things happened. He asked me if I had had any night sweats and hair loss—I'd had both. Then he remembered he had an old login for the hospital computer system as he had worked there several years earlier. He was able to hack into the system and look at my X-rays.

'The result was that he suddenly became very concerned. I was to go straight back to the hospital for urgent blood tests and a chest X-ray. He told me my broken shoulder could end up being the best thing that had ever happened to me and that I wasn't to go home or stop off anywhere, but to go directly to the hospital. When I asked him about making an appointment to get the results, he told me not to worry about that. "You're my priority now," he said with an anxious look on his face.

'I must admit I panicked a bit as I left the surgery. I walked to the hospital – half an hour's walk on the ice trying not to slip over on my bad shoulder – and was in quite a state by the time I got there.

'It wasn't until later that evening that I asked Mum to pray with me and I realised God was bigger than the situation. Two days later one of the girls at church informed me that she wanted to pray for my shoulder. When I told her about the "lump" situation, she and another guy laid hands on me and prayed. We agreed together that the lump would be gone and for an increase of faith and health.'

I was stunned by her story and did not know what to say. How could this be happening to someone so young and beautiful. The cold weather continued unabated, and it was some time before I heard from Joy again.

'How are you, Joy? Have you had any results?' I asked, hardly daring to hear the answer.

She continued her story.

'My blood tests came a few days later and were normal – this more or less ruled out conditions such as leukaemia. Five days later my chest X-ray came back, again clear. The next step is to get a biopsy of the lump and to have it removed. My doctor has made an urgent appointment with the ear, nose and throat clinic at the hospital and I will be seen within two weeks (pretty miraculous considering the epic waiting lists).'

The two weeks seemed to drag. I couldn't stop thinking about her and realised that for Joy it would seem like eternity. Eventually the time passed and I contacted her again. My heart raced as she updated me.

'When I went to the appointment the consultant asked me some questions and then fed a camera up my nose and into my throat. He poked about for a bit and then withdrew the camera. He then studied my X-rays again for some minutes.

"There's no lump there now," he said as he turned back to me, looking slightly perplexed. "Whatever it was has gone. There is no need to come back to see me as there is definitely no cancer."

'God is good!' She added.

I was too overwhelmed to reply. That had to be an understatement.

The family on dad's 100th birthday in July 2008
Standing: Enid, me, Henry, Susy, Tom, Chris, Joy, Stephen, Rebecca, Pete, James and Fiona
Sitting: John (friend), Dad, Mum, Dilys

Chapter Sixteen

Christmas

It was on December the twelfth in 2010 that my dad passed away. He was one hundred and two years old, and was ready to go. The last six months had been difficult for him, for my mother (who was ninety four) and for my sister, Dilys, who lived next door to them in Neyland, Pembrokeshire. He had needed twenty four hour care as he began to deteriorate, and when his ability to swallow even liquidised food was lost, we knew it was the end. He passed away peacefully in the night, in his own bed. This is what he wanted. Mum and Dilys looked after him to the end, with carers calling in three times a day. When he was unable to swallow liquids, my mother would wipe gauze soaked in pineapple juice around his mouth to keep it moist. He had lived a long and fulfilled life and had touched many lives on his way through, judging by the number of heart-felt letters that dropped onto mum's doormat.

The funeral was arranged for December the

seventeenth at Narberth crematorium. The weather was terrible and the roads treacherous with the ice and snow. All my children and their partners were staying over night at a Travelodge near by. They arrived at various hours throughout the night, having worked all day. Pete had the furthest to come as he had to drive all the way from Leeds, but he arrived about the same time as Susy and Tom from Bristol. James and Fiona had had their work's Christmas party in Cheltenham that evening and arrived in the early hours of the next morning. Enid's son, Stephen and his wife, Rebecca, were travelling down from Bristol with Joy and Chris who had come from Liverpool. They were leaving Bristol at half past six on the Friday morning to make sure that they arrived in time for the ten forty-five funeral.

Enid, Henry and I were already in Neyland and did what we could to comfort mum in her loss. She had been with dad for seventy years, sixty eight of those in marriage. He would leave a large hole in her life.

On the Thursday evening we had a telephone call from the funeral director.

'The local weather forecast says that Narberth is going to have eight inches of snow over night. The crematorium will be shut. I'm afraid the funeral will have to be postponed.'

This was dreadful news.

'When will we be able to have it?' asked mum.

'I'm afraid that the next available slot is Christmas Eve.'

This was so inconvenient for everyone as they were even now battling against the elements to get here. We could not let it happen.

'We will have to pray that the snow will give Narberth a miss,' commented Enid.

So we did. We prayed that the snow would move away and not fall on Narberth before the funeral. And we all went off to bed so that we would be rested for the next day.

In the morning the phone rang. It was the funeral director again.

'You know that snow that was forecast?' he asked. 'Well it missed Narberth, and the funeral can go ahead!'

Even though the roads were still covered in ice and snow, many people braved the elements to attend the Quaked funeral and say goodbye to dad. It was a time of celebration for his life as well as the sadness of his death. It was followed by a light buffet in a pub near bye for all the brave souls who had attended the funeral. In the evening we had a delicious meal for all the family in the Jolly Sailor restaurant, dad's favourite eating place, with amazing views over the river Cleddau and it's bridge. Dad would have approved.

* * *

When we returned to Chard on the Sunday, only two lanes of the motorway were open because of the snow. Everyone was driving very cautiously and we made it home safely. The house was bitterly cold when we walked in and we turned on the heating straight away, then walked out to the back garden to see whether the tank had had a filling of oil. It had not.
We had oil central heating and we had not had a top up since February. Usually the company tops us up at the beginning of autumn and then again in the new year. But not this year. So in November, before the start of the cold weather, we sent them one of their own cards to say we needed a delivery of oil as we were only a quarter full. A week later, as we had no response, I phoned them and left a message on their answer phone. Another week later I did the same. Then sent an e-mail. Still nothing.

On the Monday of Christmas week, after returning from the funeral, I made another phone call to them. This time I got through to their headquarters. The lady was very pleasant and told me that we were scheduled to have a filling in January.

'That's no good!' I exclaimed. 'We'll have run out by then!'

'Well the drivers are very busy at the moment because of the bad weather and they're doing their best. I'll pass on your message to the depot,' she assured me.

By now there was only a little bit of oil left at the

bottom of the tank. If it was to last until January we would have to be very sparing with it.

'We'd better turn off the heating to conserve the remains of the oil so we can eke it out over Christmas when we shall have all the family here,' Henry said.

I agreed.

We turned off the heating, lit the two old paraffin heaters, plugged in our electric fire and added some more clothes to our already overloaded bodies. It was not enough to warm us up.

On Tuesday I phoned the company again. The lady tried to put me through to the depot but they were engaged.

'They'll call you back,' she promised.

They did not.

Wednesday I managed to get through to the depot. I pleaded with them.

'Sorry,' was their reply. 'All the tanker drivers are too busy at the moment.'

Thursday I spoke to them again.

'Actually, one of our tanker drivers did attempt to drive down your road yesterday,' she explained. 'But there was a car covered in snow, abandoned in the road and the driver couldn't get past. We did try.'

I ran down the road to have a look. There it was. It had obviously not moved since the snow had fallen. It was outside the bungalow that was being lived in by the

Portuguese men. Perhaps the owner had gone back to Portugal for Christmas and had just left it there. I was filled with woe! Henry and I discussed what we could do. We drove down to Focus and bought two more electric heaters.

On Friday (Christmas Eve) we decided we would ask the police to move the car (not very likely, I know!) so I walked round the corner to read the number plate.

The car had gone! Disappeared! The road was empty!

I tried phoning the depot again, but it was engaged.

'We will have to pray,' said Henry. 'There's nothing else we can do now.'

I agreed and went into the sitting room to petition my heavenly Father.

After a little while I opened my eyes and could not believe what I saw as I looked out of the window! Was it a mirage? There was a petrol tanker just leaving the front of our house. I leapt up, calling to Henry as I tried to put my shoes and coat on in a hurry. I was going to go out and give the tanker driver such a big kiss! Unfortunately, I did not reach him in time and he drove off into the distance.

It was the best Christmas present we could have had and the 'whoosh' of the central heating as it leapt into life was music to our ears!

Henry and I after 40 years of marriage